BEAUTIFULLY

Graced

When Grace Takes Over the Impossible

ASHLEY J. DARLING

BEAUTIFULLY *Graced*
Copyright ©2017 Ashley Darling

Butterfly with a heart on frontal wing on side view icon made by Freepik from www.flaticon.com

Unless otherwise stated, all Scripture quotations are taken from the *Holy Bible*, New Living Translation, copyright © 1996, 2004, 2015 by Tyndale House Foundation. Used by permission of Tyndale House Publishers, Inc., Carol Stream, Illinois 60188.

All rights reserved. No part of this publication may be reproduced or transmitted in any form or by any means, either electronically or mechanically including photocopying, recording, or by any information storage and/or retrieval system, without the expressed written permission of the publisher.

ISBN 978-0-9991896-6-5 (paperback edition)

ALL RIGHTS RESERVED

Printed in the U.S.A.

To Him who wrote my life's story, and graced me with this opportunity to share my testimony, thank you. Thank you for choosing me as your vessel to be a tangible witness of your grace and love; my life has never been the same since I said 'Yes' to your will.

Christopher, my husband, my best friend, my biggest supporter, thank you for reading my 'thoughts' in my notebook and encouraging me to put my testimony and truth into a book. Thank you for challenging me daily to seek God wholeheartedly as I allowed Him to pour into me. I love the fact that you love God first and that your whole aim is to be forever pleasing in His sight, this makes it easy to love me and our children. I appreciate the nights you fed and watched our babies as I spent time studying and writing; I love you.

To my sweet and energetic blessings, Christopher and Carys, thank you for always reminding me that I'm not just doing this for myself, but for you both, in the hope that when you get older, you're encouraged to live for Jesus. Thank you, my loves, for being a part of my 'grace' in human form.

My parents, Byron and Rhonda, my sisters Le'Ronda, Mya and Sy'Rai, your love and your support throughout this process has been more than enough!

My 'Garnet's Girls' and my best friend, Yasmin, I love you so much. You believed in this. You believed in me. I'll never forget how you've made me feel during this process. Malikah Pinder and Laquisha Wallace, the ladies who saw this before I could ever think it, the daily texts to remind me of purpose helped me to birth this book. Thank you for your love and your obedience to God as you spoke over my life what He released to you concerning me.

Contents

Introduction 9

Part One:
My Story: From Despair to Hope

The Beginning 15

Seemingly Picture Perfect 17

Broken Beyond Repair 24

Faith vs. Reality 27

The Desert Experience 35

Ready, Set, Fight! 41

He Put the Pieces Back Together 47

White Flag 51

Purpose and Grace 57

Part Two
Your Turn: Encounter Grace

God Will Make You Laugh! 67

Vulnerable, Again! 73

The Bounce Back 77

Guarding Your Heart and Mind 83

The Cross 89

The Butterfly Effect 95

Conclusion 101

Your story doesn't just end at your mistake or your situation. It doesn't end with you giving up. Your story has grace written all over it; your story has been written by the Master himself. Go ahead and trust Him with the next chapter in your life, I dare you.

Signed,

From one beautifully graced woman to another.

Introduction

I've always had a plan for my life. At every age, I had a goal I desired to accomplish. I can see it clearly, scribbled in my journal. At twenty-one I wrote about how semi-independent I'd be, with my own car, doing my studies abroad and living in my own apartment. I even mentioned the type of friends I'd possibly have. At twenty-five, I saw myself working my dream job in the hospitality field, traveling the world alongside my significant other, whom I would have gotten together with at the age of twenty-three or so. Children weren't penciled in until thirty-three, neither was marriage. All my thoughts, plans, and aspirations were written down; that was the thing to do. The plan was to mark off each goal as I completed them.

However, as you may have guessed, those years of my life didn't go as perfectly and on target as I had thought. I couldn't just tear the page out of my journal and say, 'Here, God, this is what I want for my life. This'll work. I think it's perfect. Just make this happen.' In my journal, I didn't leave room for God. I didn't leave room for life to occur. I envisioned a perfect world with no headaches or setbacks, nothing but extreme happiness. The truth is that our journey is never easy going where we just skip through the tulip fields of life, and we encounter no tests, no trials, and the grass is always green. Our stories may differ, but each of our journeys is just that; one that may be filled with trials and heartache. There'll be days when you're dressed from head to toe with a smile, and on others, you may have to drag yourself out of bed. No matter where you may be right now, your journey is purpose-filled. Over time, you'll see how you've blossomed. Those pieces that were once shameful to expose will become the very pieces of you that you become proud to share with others so they can know how amazing God's grace is. He takes the messiest parts of our lives and creates

Introduction

something so beautiful. While we journey to purpose, God is always beside us imparting wisdom to us and showering us with His love. I wholeheartedly believe that incredible things happen when grace takes over.

In this book, I share my personal journey of overcoming depression and insecurity during my Christian walk. I'm writing in hopes that it encourages you not to give up, and not to accept defeat. I'm writing to tell you that it is possible to survive what you're going through once you decide to walk with God all the way. He's graced us for this journey; His strength swallows up our weakness and pushes us to keep going. His Grace never leaves us.

Part One

My Story:

From Despair to Hope

Chapter One
The Beginning

For years, I envisioned how I'd want to be proposed to and what the perfect scenery would be, and my husband hit the nail right on the head. After the tears had stopped flowing and the congratulations lulled, I curiously asked myself, "now what?" We had decided on a date, the venue, our bridal party, the colours, the flowers, the caterer and even designed the cake, but there was still a void. We, or better still, I was so wrapped up in the wedding day and increasingly long guest list that I did not apprehend the severity of my then fiancé slipping his ring onto my finger. I was beyond smitten with becoming Mrs. Ashley Darling. So smitten that I had already begun to lose myself.

A few weeks after the betrothal, we began counselling; this is where all truth and nothing but the truth was laid out on the table. Each counselling session acted as a mirror, not only for our relationship but for me as well. Challenged to find my true self and open up about past hurts and potential pain is where I found myself occasionally during the sessions. The truth is, I had experienced dysfunctional and emotionally draining relationships before my then fiancé. And since I'm being honest, at the beginning of our relationship, before the thoughts of even a future tougher, he too had been a culprit of some of those scars on my heart. A few scars on which I placed band-aids as opposed to allowing forgiveness and healing. So, yes, there I was with my wedding colours picked out and the silhouette of the perfect dress in mind. But my scars that had yet to heal properly began to ooze because the priest was getting deep and thorough about my life.

In our lives, no matter how much red bottoms we own and how much 'life's good' selfies we take and post on social media, we find ourselves being the recipient of hurt. It is inevitable; no matter how cautious we claim to be, at some point we are faced with it. However, it is what we do after the hurt has rendered us seemingly exposed and powerless that counts. Are we willing to allow grace to take over? Or do we just band aid whatever hurt we have and allow 'time to heal all wounds?'

Seemingly Picture Perfect

Our wedding was talked about for weeks. We were both saved and expected to blossom and bloom both in church and our community. We were the 'picture perfect' couple, many would say. Many people held us in high esteem. They confidently called us the 'Power Couple' of this generation. We'd smile and humbly accept because we had a great desire to create change within our community. We had no clue what was about to hit us, and hard, too.

Soon after the honeymoon, my thoughts of being that power couple was put on hold. Chris and I came from two totally different worlds. I came from an affluent nuclear family, while he, on the other hand, came from a struggling single parent home where his mom played the roles of mother, father, and breadwinner. We each did things differently, and our perception of marriage and the examples around us were distant. That bliss that they promised for months after the wedding day quickly faded. Like any newlywed couple, we had challenges, and we fought. Neither of us had a personal vehicle, so we had to rely on the company's truck as a means to get around. Yes, a big flatbed truck that took us wherever we needed to go. If that wasn't terrible enough, Chris has built our home solely independently, and when I say that, I mean we were not connected to the power company, the water company or the telephone company. Our house ran on a solar system, and we relied on the sun to provide us with power and the rain to provide us with water, and when that didn't happen, we toted water from various taps. Yes, this girl who came from having it all was brought into the situation where there was little to nothing. Our finances were the cause of many fights. I expected my husband to be the provider that my father was as soon as we got married. I knew I didn't marry a man with a silver spoon in his mouth, but my thoughts weren't there during counselling and before the wedding bells rang. I was still stuck on my Vera Wang gown and my Swarovski crystals to ever think deeply about the 'what ifs.'

We fought for weeks at a time, about finances, church, and family. I remember thinking that I made a huge mistake in saying "yes" and "I do." Some of our fights would even result in us using foul language toward one another. There were times when we would go to church not even talking to one another. I'd be on the praise team, and he in the congregation, but no one would know we had issues. We kept our lives 'picture perfect'. I didn't know what else to do. Our fights were not always dealt with, which lead to even substantial ones later on. I refused to go to anyone and express what I was feeling because I had not seen any other married couples doing it. They made everything look so easy. I started to think that my marriage was the doomed one because everyone looked so unblemished; so perfect. I'd hear 'marriage isn't a bed of roses,' but that was all that they said. No one shared their testimonies; no one offered to be candid with me about how marriage really was. They all just showed me 'perfection,' and that perfection is exactly what I strived for. Because of my thinking, I rated my marriage and my husband. I would compare him to the woman whose husband bought flowers, and jewellery and cooked for her and displayed it all on social media. I didn't think that marriage took a lot of work and that nothing happens overnight. I wanted change, NOW. I wanted to be happy, NOW. But I wasn't getting that NOW solution, and that was the problem. Our marriage was slowly falling apart; our happy days became days filled with anger and sadness. Our friendship became a once was. We were living as strangers, and we bottled up our feelings. It was like walking on egg shells. The tension between us was so thick, everyone at work knew when things weren't good at home. We just existed. We didn't read together; we didn't pray together. We were going through a tough time in our lives and marriage. I had no idea how to merge lanes with my husband. You see, we both were on the same highway, moving at different speeds in separate lanes. We didn't operate as a unit. I did my thing, and he did his. We were so green to this whole marriage thing.

By the time we were in our second year of marriage, we had mastered the art of faking it. We didn't express ourselves to anyone while we were going through those extremely trying times. Our lives looked so perfect for Facebook and social media. Then our son came along. He acted like a band-aid for all our problems. We began to focus all our attention, time and love into this new being that brought us great joy.

Nevertheless, like any cut that hasn't been tended to, but bandaged up, it began to bleed…again. Our fights began with my husband not doing enough, in my eyes, for our son. I argued with him about getting up with me to tend to the baby. We argued about buying pampers and milk and clothes for our growing boy. I wasn't used to being in the place where I had to ask for things. I had watched my parents for years, my father was the provider and protector of our home, so I knew what a man was supposed to do for his family. This was all new to me. I took offense over every little thing, and I didn't realize how deep of a hole I was digging. I wasn't willing to hear excuses or explanations. I started to get miserable and annoyed with everything around me.

I kept repeating to myself over and over that I had gotten married too fast. I kept thinking, "you knew you weren't ready for this. This is for life; you're bound, and there is no way you can get out!" Those thoughts surged through my mind and resentment of November 30th, 2013, started to set in. The perfect life I had envisioned was beginning to look not so perfect after all. I had watched people get married, and within months they were already separated, and onto new relationships like they never made vows before God. 'This isn't what I signed up for,' I kept telling myself. I could've been finishing college, or at my dream job; but here I was playing wife, in a marriage where the husband and I had stopped kissing and loving on one another. We were living like roommates. It was business as usual for us. This isn't the life I had planned out in my head. This isn't how it should be. This wasn't the perfect life I had dreamt about when I was younger.

On our wedding anniversary, I sat on our upstairs deck overlooking the ocean with tears in my eyes. The thought of going another year while everything was going wrong pricked my heart. I was in this for life, and November 30th reminded me of that. I felt so frustrated, so defeated. We were still fighting and not talking to one another. I was crying and asking God why He allowed me to get married since this was obviously the wrong move and nothing was going right. At that point, I didn't see the purpose in my marriage. I didn't see us being that perfect power couple that everyone bragged about in church. I had already checked out of my marriage emotionally and mentally. I felt an intense regret, and I couldn't get over it. I retreated.

Broken Beyond Repair

I couldn't let anyone know what was going on. I was too ashamed. I believed that my marriage was the only marriage going through difficult times and that we were the only ones fighting day in and day out. We fought as if we were enemies and not on the same team or in the same boat with one another; we were both sinking. Being the emotional person, I would hold in whatever my husband did to me; I wouldn't release. I had no clue on how to release and forgive and show grace. That wasn't on my list, nor was I interested in learning how to carry it out. So, there I was married, saved, on the praise team and I was full of bandages. If my husband offended me, I'd stop talking, and band-aid my hurt. So, every time I was offended and hurt, I'd slap on a band –aid by getting offensive and shutting him out. Then I would go about my not so normal life.

As Christians, we've learnt how to master the art of covering up. We've mastered this so well that it has been embedded into our genetic makeup. I thought no one could handle my truth so I concealed those parts that weren't so beautiful; the hurt and the pain. The church is supposed to be for the lost, the hopeless, and the broken; why is it filled with perfect beings, who have never sinned or have never had issues in life? I was saved and covered with bandages and issues that I had no clue existed. I unconsciously became one of those people who didn't trust God with my issues. I didn't give it over to him to heal and restore. I refused to face my truth, and I was ashamed to allow anyone handle what had become my truth. I felt as if I was in a dark room, with no way out, the walls closing in. Just me and what had become my life, haunting me. I quickly became a shell of a person. All of my issues and problems started to take over my life, my personality. Instead of calling me 'Ash,' I'd answer to 'emotionally distressed.' Instead of calling me 'Ashley,' I'd answer to 'broken soul.' This is where I was. I had become this broken person. So, broken, I didn't even recognize myself, this was now my life. Being broken robs us of so much. Our truth is hidden behind the scars, the fear, and the negative thinking. We don't quickly give our truth to anyone, even if they are sincere in helping us. Therefore, we hide; we hide behind our makeup, then we sit so perfectly, like figurines on a coffee table. This was me, so broken but dressed impeccably. I wasn't whole; I was in pieces. I was so broken; no one could fix me. I couldn't even fix me. I didn't know where to start. Have you ever been there? Or is it just me? I was at the very bottom. I could literally feel myself slipping deep into depression. I was drowning. I had no help; I didn't allow myself to be helped. I couldn't tell you what was next for me. I couldn't tell you how I'd bounce back, or even if I would. Depression swallowed me up, and I had no fight to combat it. I was a walking time bomb, at any minute I could blow up. I knew I wasn't whole, and I was doing nothing about it. Healing was so far from me. I was vulnerable, and anything could attack me, and I'd give in to the attack. I couldn't think, I alienated myself, and I felt offended by the simplest things. I had become an emotional wreck. I was the perfect candidate for the enemy to take up residence in.

Chapter Two

Faith vs. Reality

I knew I was in too deep when I couldn't feel God; we had become like strangers. I read the Bible a little here and there, and I watched church on television instead of going. Church had become so traditional. They talked about blessings and favour, but being broken that wasn't something I needed to hear every Sunday. My time was spent working and being mommy to my newborn son. I did not realize how far I'd drifted away from God. My husband and I had active ministries before getting married, D.I.M.E and K.J.4.L. D.I.M.E (Daughters Who Inspire, Motivate and Empower) was birthed after seeing so many young women and girls in my community struggle with knowing their worth. I had seen dozens of promising young girls become statistics because they had little to no assurance of how valuable they truly are. D.I.M.E emerged in hopes of reassuring young girls of God's love and his plans for their lives. K.J.4.L, King Jesus 4 Life, was birthed by my husband as a discipleship program, for those newly saved, and those young in the faith. His aim was to help people get saved and remain saved. These ministries were so active and effective, we hosted events and constantly did outreach, but our drive and passion became a thing of the past. The ministry I'd started seemed covered in cobwebs. I had already become one of those Christians who had gotten lukewarm. Scary, I know, but at the time, it didn't bother me. I allowed my situation to dictate to me. It took pre-eminence over the word of God. But I knew something was different. I was changing. I found myself always on edge, ready to snap at whoever offended me or 'loaned' me their 'advice.' Depression, fear, and anger quickly became a part of my persona. The husband that I prayed to God earnestly for became an enemy to me. I made him my enemy. I just couldn't catch myself. The truth is, I no longer had a relationship with God. I was barely clinging to the worship music I had downloaded on my cell phone and the daily scriptures that chimed in on my phone by the Bible App. I was just there, just existing. I had no clue what my next move would be, but He did.

   I sat in the bathroom as tears stung my eyes. I can still taste the saltiness of the water as it left my bloodshot eyes and trickled onto my lips. My heart was racing so fast I started to shake. Immediately, fear and anger surged throughout my shaking body. I stared at the two pink lines, totally speechless. I was about to be a mommy to a second child. I couldn't think straight, but I managed to let '…God, please take this baby back,' depart from my lips. I felt no remorse in saying it because here I was newly married and broken. I'd recently turned twenty-four and already a mother to my four-month-old son. All my adult life, I had taken 'control,' but this was out of my hands. I hated not being able to have the final say. I mean, there was another option, but that wasn't an option. After sharing with my close family and friends, they all said the same thing "...oh, stop worrying so much, they'll grow up together" or "...it's good to have them close together, to get it over with..." but those words, were no comfort to me at all. At the time, I was getting little to no sleep, and the thought of taking care of baby number two seemed daunting. As directed by my mom, I made an appointment with my gynaecologist, and he did a test, and that too was positive, so then came a scan. There was a sack, but nothing in it. I breathed a huge sigh of relief, and he advised me that I may miscarry but that I should come back in a few weeks for another scan. I know you may be thinking how crazy I am, right? Being able to have children when some people could only dream of seeing those two pink lines. Simply put, I could not see the 'blessing' in this 'blessing.' I wanted to have a handle on my life. I wanted to be able to say "yea or nay." I was so relieved by what the doctor said, I didn't even think about possibly being pregnant anymore because I clung to his words that I would 'miscarry.' I followed his orders and went back for a scan, and there it was. Heart beating strong and floating around like it was always there. I cried, right then and there in his office. I didn't know what I would do with two babies under two years old. Both in Pampers, both sucking from a bottle, both mine. I couldn't wrap the thought around my head that I would be the mother of two babies, who would be exactly thirteen months apart. I began to panic. What would I do? How would their feeding schedules work? What about financially taking care of these babies? Buying an extra case of Pampers, and milk, and clothes and bottles, and insurance. It was all just too much for my mind to comprehend. At this point, Jeremiah 29:11 "For I know the plans I have for you," declares the Lord. "Plans to prosper you and not to harm you, plans to give you hope and a future," was no comfort to me at all. I wanted to believe that His plans are always prosperous and hopeful. I desired to see in the future, that everything would work out and that there was a purpose for this happening in my life. A friend of mine lives by the motto "Seasons and Reasons." I know that everything operates seasonally and that there are reasons for everything happening under the sun. I just couldn't see my "Seasons and Reasons."

As the weeks went by, my feelings became more and more mixed, and I stayed on edge. I started to snap at my husband for the tiniest things, and I became irate with God because he didn't comply with my request. I refused to read my Bible or pray, subconsciously thinking I was punishing God when I was only punishing myself. Have you ever been there? Or, is it just me? Have you ever been so angry with God for the things that are going on around you? You're angry because you feel that He should be having your best interest at heart. Sometimes we figure that our way is always best and that God's unknown plans for our lives may be too risky to rely on. Proverbs 3:5 "Trust in the Lord with all thine heart, and lean not unto thine own understanding." We've heard this time after time, but while we are in our situations, this may be hard to accept. I did not trust Him because reality fought with my faith. It seemed like everything was going downhill, and fast.

I'm usually one to take care of myself, but I wasn't even doing that. I had gained weight because I was eating any and everything. I didn't care how I dressed, and I was ashamed of my rapidly growing belly. I started to worry about what people would say about me. I got the stares and the looks and the 'boy, you didn't waste any time, you're pregnant again?!' It was so embarrassing. I felt like I had gone from being this person whom others admired to being someone no one really cares about. There were people whom I had graduated with who already had businesses, degrees, great paying jobs and 'living life' through traveling and creating memories. But there I was, pregnant with baby number two and not even twenty-five yet. I started to compare my life to those women I saw on social media. They seemingly had it all together; the perfect house, the perfect husband and marriage, their dream jobs and perfect bodies. I couldn't see the city from the smoke even if I wanted to, as my mom would say. I was struggling. I had no drive. I was too busy looking at and coveting the lives of other Christian women neglecting the fact that I too could work toward bettering myself and my life.

Chapter Three
The Desert Experience

The more I thought about my situation, the more depressed I became. I didn't know who I was. I didn't know what life had in store for me anymore. When I left home after high school, I enrolled in college and studied Hospitality Management. I dreamt of opening my own hotel or owning rental properties and being super successful. I still do have that dream. But, every time I thought about being a wife and mother of two babies, my dreams went out the window and so did my hope and faith. I had become disgruntled, and I was encountering the desert experience that I heard so many Christians talk about. I still had no one to talk to, because I felt like no one would be able to understand. I did not trust my wounds to anyone because I had been burned before. So there, in one of lowest times of my life, I was alone. Every seemingly genuine person, I pushed away in fear of being victimized by their words and their thoughts about my life. I had never felt so far from God before in my life. But it was my fault. I had pushed Him away with my thoughts and words. The days seemed so long, and week after week I struggled with the decision to either go to church or not. Church just seemed like a past time, a ritual. I couldn't 'feel' God no matter how hard I sang, no matter how many times tears streamed down my face. I was in the desert, all alone.

After months of not feeling God, I started to doubt the very purpose of my existence. The only thoughts I had was that I'm a wife and soon to be mom of two babies. I thought my life was just that. Those thoughts alone sent me spiralling into depression. I had heard of depression and people battling with it, but I never gave much thought to it at all, until it hit home for me. Depression is real. It's not something that is wanted or invited into a person's life. Depression tends to control the life of its host. It causes you to be filled with doubts and the what ifs about life. When I was younger, I had my life planned 'perfectly,' and as of that moment, I had taken another course. When I thought about how quickly my life had changed, and how 'imperfect' it seemed to me, I was careening head-on with depression. As humans, we automatically take on the role of planning our lives; from deciding where we go to college, where we're going to live and what major we desire to take up in school. In most cases, this is not all bad. Ambition is good. However, when our lives do not turn out as we've hoped, then what? Being in a place with no one around but utter silence is the breeding ground for hopelessness. I had no hope, no joy, no peace and most importantly, my faith was at an all-time low; it was reading 'negative.' I then understood how Jacob felt. He went for years in silence; He couldn't hear from God. It's amazing how we expect God to talk to us when we've shut Him out. We haven't invited Him in totally, yet we want Him to open the floodgates over our lives. It took me a while to understand that not praying, not spending time with God led me into the desert that I'm speaking about, and that is just what the enemy wanted. I was helping him, and I didn't even know it. Once the devil can get you at your weakest point, he strikes, and before you know it, you're second-guessing God and your purpose, like I did. Then, retreating to your old lifestyle is inevitable. You end up fornicating, drinking, partying and committing every sin that Jesus once saved you from. This is where the devil wants you, vulnerable. Here, he can attack you every way possible; physically, mentally, emotionally, you name it.

John 10:10, "The thief comes to only to steal and kill and destroy..." He comes to steal your joy and your peace, he comes to kill your purpose, and he comes to destroy your faith. My faith at this point wasn't even the size of a mustard seed. I was so miserable; I had no idea what was in store for me. I could not please God faithless, and therefore, my desert experience became even worse. Being without God is being miserable, especially when you once had a relationship with Him. You find yourself hostile toward everyone and everything. My walk with God had become stagnant. But then again, was I even walking at all? Being in a place where you're all alone and emotionless can either make you weak until you eventually break or it can strengthen you, so you come out stronger than before. But, don't you need God for that?

Chapter Four

Ready, Set, Fight!

Fighting is inevitable, but what we do once we're confronted with the fight is what makes the world of difference. No matter how many times I read about Jacob in Genesis 32:22, I am amazed at his desire to be blessed by God. This desire pushed him to fight for what mattered most to him. The last time Jacob heard from God was before his arrival to Paddan Aram, where he was married to Leah and Rachel. Throughout his journey of working for Laban and marrying his daughters and having children, we have yet to see where Jacob heard from God. Hence the importance of his wrestling with God for a blessing. Jacob was tired of his 'desert experience' so he took full advantage of that one encounter with God and indeed came out blessed.

While in your dry place, you feel defeated and weak. You feel so confused that you don't know what to do. Fighting may seem like the last resort, but, can I tell you that fighting is your only resort. As much as I knew I had to fight, I felt like I couldn't. I felt like I didn't have the strength to fight. I had allowed the enemy to whisper so many lies in my head until they become truth etched in my mind.

Within months, my world was filled with double bottles, double pampers, double feedings. I didn't have time to think. I started going back to church and envy flooded my space. There were women doing what I once was doing before I had my children, and I was just there, measuring out formula for baby bottles. I cried out so loud to God. I was empty. Completely empty and humble. I knew that there was a work for me to do. I knew I had a purpose. I remember asking God for forgiveness for all the nasty and unacceptable thoughts that I allowed to cloud my mind. I purposefully asked Him for an encounter with

Him, so that I'd know if He still had work for me to do, if I was still 'chosen'. I was so insecure. I wasn't connected to Him like I used to be, and this is where the enemy crept in and whispered those lies I so gullibly believed. I clearly remember him saying that my husband and I were mismatched because he heard from God and I didn't. I foolishly believed that and I kept drawing away from my husband more, and more. I hardly laughed with my husband and I refused to share things with him like I used to, and then the loneliness got bigger, because I had no one to share my fears with. I isolated myself from everyone because I didn't feel adequate. I had the picture-perfect family, but I was dealing with stuff that I feared sharing. I was afraid to share my truth, because I'd heard that people in church cannot handle the true you, so don't air your dirty laundry. I'd started to copy some of the women I saw every Sunday; 'going through' but dressed up, made up, hair fixed, shoes, bags, and dresses all matched, but you would never know because they hid it so well. They literally faked it; some hurt for years, but afraid to be that one to show weakness. I started to get so tired feeling the doubts flood my mind. I was getting fed up with the fear, loneliness and insecurities; they were taking over my life. I was inches away from erupting, from totally giving up. I realized that I had to fight! I had to fight for my life, for peace and joy in my marriage. I had to fight for my son and daughter. I didn't want them to grow up having a bitter mother. I wanted them to be proud to call me their mom. Truth be told, my greatest fight came because of them. The minute I decided to fight is when Jesus stepped in. I was at my breaking point, no other resort, and His grace stepped in and took over.

Psalms 51:17 says "The sacrifices of God are a broken spirit; a broken and contrite heart, O God, you will not despise." I needed to get to that point for my breakthrough, for my total healing. I could not do it on my own. I could not do it without His grace. His grace needed to take over my life, and transform me. Our brokenness speaks volumes to Him. Just like Hannah, I had to get to a place of total emptiness, a place where all I needed was for Him to take control. I had to be willing and fully surrendered for Him to do His work. Our weakness, to Him, says without You, I am nothing. His grace, His perfect grace gives us the strength to continue this thing called life. It gives us the courage to face the things we could not do on our own. It gives us the bravery to confront the devil one-on-one and take back what is rightfully ours; our mind, our peace, or families, whatever the enemy might have taken, we can boldly approach him and say "Hey you, I've come for my stuff, give it back!" His grace gives us that opportunity, and it reminds us that He is always fighting for us. He is seated on the right hand of the Father, fighting for and advocating for us. His grace urges us to seek Him, daily; seeking God means that we search earnestly for Him. We seek His presence; through the word, worship and prayer. 1st Timothy 2:3-4 "This is good, and pleases God our saviour, who wants all people to be saved and to come to a knowledge of the truth." He desires to have a relationship with us and that our lives be lived abundantly in Him; His grace leaves room for just that.

Chapter Five
He Put the Pieces Back Together

As insecurity, fear, and loneliness became the puzzle pieces to my life, my God decided to step in and transform what had become my normal. The metamorphosis had begun. When I was eighteen, I decided to get a tattoo. It was a random act, so I had no clue what I was going to get. I had no favourites, but when I got to the parlour, I fell in love with the butterfly samples. I wasn't a huge fan of them before, but I got it inked on my right shoulder. The minute God was getting ready to do a work in my life, was when I was reminded of the tattoo I would usually forget I even had. But, like the butterfly, I was about to be transformed.

As I began to make God the centre of everything in my life again, by spending time, and praying and reading His word, the weights that once had me bound began to lift. The parts of me that were once dead came to life again. He started to piece back all those things I knew were once broken and even some of the things I never gave much thought to. It would be amiss of me to even give the illusion that at the snap of a finger all the things I had lost came back quickly. Every day was a step in the right direction, though. I had issues, deep rooted ones that I had no idea were there. I'd scroll through social media and wonder, why can't my hair be like hers, or why can't my body be like hers? Insecurity was implanted in me. I never thought that I was enough. I never thought that I'd measure up to these people I had seen on social media. These were my pieces; insecurity, mistrust, hate and an unforgiving spirit. My pieces were big. Big enough to take over my life and make me bitter and angry and displeasing to God.

"The acts of the flesh are obvious: sexual immorality, impurity, and debauchery; idolatry and witchcraft; hatred, discord, jealousy, fits of rage, selfish ambition, dissension, factions and envy…I warn you as I did before, that those who live like this will not inherit the kingdom of God." The thought of that alone now scares me. I was nowhere close to fully being God's own. I was far from hitting the mark; but He graced me to have another chance at life with Him, abundantly. Those broken and shameful pieces, Jesus dusted them off and pieced them together for me. No longer were my pieces labelled warped and misfits. Through the process, I've learned just how beautiful being broken is. Of course, the feeling is one less desired, but overall, there is beauty in being broken. The woman with the issue of blood is one of my absolute favourite Bible stories. A woman suffered from her issue for twelve years, and no one could heal her. Doctor after doctor, year after year and nothing changed. Then she heard about Jesus, and she got desperate. I could imagine her feelings, her longing to be made whole. Sometimes, we feel that being different from others is a curse. We find ourselves asking God why we're made this way, or why things in our lives couldn't be different. But, in most cases, our difference is purposeful in His sight. Just imagine, she had been dealing with this for so long, so she pushed through the crowd and touched him; vulnerable and broken. She didn't care that everyone would know her secret. Back in the day, a bleeding woman would be rejected. It was imperative that she kept to herself because of her uncleanness; she was scorned. But she no longer cared about the rules, she just needed to be touched, by the Master, the Healer. She allowed her faith to do the talking, and she was healed. Had she not had her issue, would she had ever met Jesus? Our brokenness pushes us toward our destiny, as long as we allow the Master to do the healing. Even if you may be missing a few pieces, He's gracious enough to put them back together for you.

Chapter Six

White Flag

I was three months into being a mother of two, and everything was going well. I had already learned how to balance work, two babies under the age of two, and my marriage was progressing. My husband and I began communicating more. It started with the little things, questions like 'how was your day today? Anything different happened today? Is there anything I can do for the babies if you're tired?' Then came morning when we'd get up at the same time and we began praying. We started to commit our marriage and our little family to the Lord. There were mornings where we just fell at our feet, drenched in tears, because we realized that this ministry, our marriage, and our family was bigger than all the petty stuff we put each other through, and we needed Him to grace us for our family. Then, finally, I was back to my very first love, Jesus Christ. I was reading, praying, and spending time with Him, while my eyes remained fixed on Him. The enemy was not about to let me bounce back without letting me know that he's still there, ready to take care of business.

It was my morning routine. I had just put Carys down after feeding her and changing her soiled diaper. It was about 3:30am. I drifted off to sleep and suddenly woke up with trouble breathing. Immediately, I jumped out of bed and scrambled around looking for my inhaler. It felt as though someone was snatching my breath every time I inhaled. I stumbled into the bathroom and took two puffs but I still couldn't breathe. I managed to scream for my husband with the little breath I could grasp. He heard me, and came running. My head was light, and my body felt like it was floating. I was nearly unconscious. I remember him shouting "Ashley! Ashley! Stay awake baby. Come on, stay awake! You have two children out there! Stay awake. Say Jesus. Say Jesus baby, call His name!" Five feet away from where my babies slept, death seemingly lurked around the corner. My husband was telling me to call Jesus' name, but I couldn't. I couldn't even utter my saviour's name for myself. I was rushed to the clinic where the nurse met me and she hooked me up to the oxygen tank right away. Within minutes, my breathing was regulated. The nurse looked at me bewildered and asked "…what was that all about, what just happened here?" She asked me those questions because as any asthmatic would know, that attack wasn't normal. It wasn't a regular episode. Chris and I pieced together quickly that the attack was demonic. I was just six weeks away from completing my book, and he was doing his very best to shut me up, discourage me, and push me to the side. Every time I think about it, I plug in Travis Green's song "… You made a way, when my back was against the wall, and it looked as if it was over, you made a way…" I think he thought he had me down for the count; he played my funeral in his head, but

"…Jesus saves, from the cross to the grave, Jesus saves…"

Destroying our lives is of the utmost importance for the devil, because if he can do that, he's got full control, and that would be one less person he's got to worry about spreading the gospel of Jesus Christ. We have one of those famous Bahamian sayings, that goes "dogs don't bark at parked cars." When you are not a threat for the devil, he doesn't even have you to study; you aren't a threat. The minute the enemy realizes that you've come to know how much power and authority you've got, he attacks to keep you bound and keep you from walking in your purpose. We all have a purpose; we all have a reason as to why we were born. Can you imagine hundreds of people knowing their purpose in Christ and walking in same? Can you see the army of Jesus rising? Can you? There are scores of people birthed to bring about change; there are anointed psalmists, radical preachers, prophets, books and songs that need to be written, events that need to be hosted, all for the Glory of God. But the enemy has a hold on these things; they are so lost in the world, they have no clue that they were birthed for a purpose. The enemy fights us with depression and anxiety because we cannot think for ourselves; we are emotionally unstable, we feel helpless and hopeless, and over time once they have fully taken over our lives, death is inevitable.

2 Corinthians 4:4 "Satan, who is the god of this world, has blinded the minds of those who don't believe. They are unable to see the glorious light of the Good News. They do not understand this message about the glory of Christ, who is the exact likeness of God." His aim is to keep us blind to the things of God, so we don't progress and tap into our purpose. In most cases, it is everyday life that keeps us from tapping into what God has called us to do. When we aren't caught up with working, we're caught up with making sure our homes are in order, paying bills, meeting the needs of our children, PTA meetings, and traveling etc. These things subconsciously take away from our quality time with God, whether reading His word or praying. Sometimes we may go days without opening the Bible because we're so 'busy' doing other things as opposed to being

busy for the Lord. We say that we're busy with life and we must do so much in order to live comfortably, or to make ends meet, but can you just imagine going about life without God? The enemy uses our everyday chores to distract us, to have us so caught up with making our lives 'better' until we don't even realize that we've forgotten to pray. We're so tired we don't know the last time we did early morning prayer, or when last we fasted, or when last we went to Bible study. All these are distractions from Jesus being the focus in life. A perfectly balanced life includes Jesus. Any equation with Him missing is simply imbalanced, and your life will show whether he's in your equation or not. Is he?

Chapter Seven

Purpose and Grace

While on my maternity leave, I started to write more and more. On my tablet, on pieces of paper, or even in my phone. Whatever came to mind, I wrote. For some weird reason, I had googled my daughter's name, Carys. I had the meaning of it in Turkish, which was *love* and *pleasant.* But, I decided to google her name in Greek, which is something I never did before. To my surprise, Carys means 'GRACE' in Greek. I never knew that until after I gave birth to my daughter. This blew my mind. So, I'm talking to God, in tears, and I'm like "God, you mean to tell me, Carys means GRACE? She is my example and my reminder of how good you are to me? This is the same baby I thought I couldn't handle, the same baby that I asked you to take away because it seemed overwhelming, and you helped me to name her GRACE?" My face was awash in tears, and I looked at her as she slept so peacefully. It's amazing how God gives us subtle, reminders of how good He is to us.

Throughout the Bible, we see where He reminded His own about His grace and mercy and how good He's been throughout time. When I look at my daughter, I'm reminded of how weak I once was, and how strong I've become since GRACE invaded my space. I had to have my daughter the way that I did. I had to be broken to the point of no return. I had to be at my lowest, for Him to show up during one of my humblest times in life. My purpose was birthed when I gave birth to 'Grace.' I'm blessed to be able to look Grace right in the face daily and be reminded of Him. If it had not been for Grace, I would not be writing to you. You would not hear my voice. I'd be somewhere in the background humming. For me, grace and purpose go hand in hand. I could not have achieved one, without the other. They are a part of my destiny.

We were created for a purpose. God made no mistakes in creating every human being on this earth. There are some people who knew their purpose from a certain age, and then there are others like me, who needed a little help from God by going through some stuff to recognize that there was purpose behind it all. Everyone on this earth has a reason for being born. There are times when our paths may cross, but you were born for a specific purpose, and so was I. I believe that no two people have the exact purpose, which makes each of us unique. Purpose is powerful and once you've recognized yours, you've got to grab a hold of it like you're the anchor runner in a relay race. You've got to run; run fast like Usain Bolt and start working on that purpose, building whatever it is that God has for you to do. Can you imagine leaving this world and not fulfilling your purpose, just living life as usual, and neglecting that you were born for a particular thing, and that thing was specifically for you to conquer? It grieves me to know that it took me this long to find my purpose. I'm sure I had clues all my life, but it took me a while to allow grace to introduce my purpose to me. I believe that to find and fulfil your purpose, you have to be in the right place, at the right time, for God to show up and show out in your life. Remember Saul, who became Paul after his conversion? For years, he hunted and persecuted Christians because of their faith. While on his way to carry out his vicious attacks, he was blinded by a bright light and was converted to Christianity, and became the same one who wrote hundreds of letters with instructions to Christians about how they should live for God. His purpose was fulfilled at the right place, and at the right time. He had to have been on both sides of the fence to appreciate God and what He was now doing in his life. What will it take for you to grab a hold of your purpose?

As you're introduced to your purpose and gift, it is imperative that you protect it. There are some people that the enemy uses to discourage and discredit you. Sometimes God has the most outlandish purposes and gifts for His chosen that traditional religious people cannot comprehend. It is so important that you protect your purpose and gift while developing them.

You must discern those who genuinely come to feed your spirit and those who come to sabotage the work of God. Not everyone will understand, and this is where God just 'shows off.' He says in His word that He uses the foolish to confound the wise. Can I tell you that there will be a fight, though? A fight for you to carry this purpose and birth it. There may be people who do not agree with God for choosing you. They may feel as if He should've chosen the person who was always perfect, who'd never been in a mess before to do the work that He's called you to do. But, that's just God. He uses the most unusual people to do His work. The person who had been once broken beyond repair. The person who's been best buds with GRACE and didn't even know it. Cuz' baby! When GRACE takes over your life, you don't need permission from the sister sitting next to you, the pastor or the prophet. Your grace comes from the Lord, and no one can take that away from you. Only He can if He chooses to, and He loves you too much.

    Your purpose is not just for you. Yes, you learn, and you grow in your purpose, but it's for the next generation. What we do in life affects those around us, whether we know it or not. Hence, believing in your purpose and doing what God has called you to do is important.

God has entrusted each of us with a great purpose, and it is our duty to protect it. Protecting your purpose calls for you obeying God, and to remain cautious about whom you share information with concerning your purpose or what God has called you to do. This is where being sensitive to God and His voice comes into play. He is our protector.

2 Thessalonians 3:3 "But the Lord is faithful, and he will strengthen you and protect you from the evil one." He loves us and believes in us, which is why He uses us as vessels for His glory. We have to trust Him enough to believe that He will not allow harm to come our way, but we too have to surrender ourselves and every aspect of our lives to Him. Our prayer lives must be consistent, which makes hearing from God clear as we become super sensitive to the things around us. In most cases, we then can sense those people around us who are genuinely for us and who are not. Protect your purpose.

God doesn't give you a purpose and says "Here, go." Believe me when I tell you, that you've had the 'know-how' on how to work your purpose from the day you were born, but you didn't have a clue. When you've been introduced to your purpose, your intuition on how to work this beautiful thing that God gave you starts to bloom. Like me, you begin got say "Oh! That's why I'm like this or this is why I like to do such and such!" It has been in our genetic makeup from our mother's womb. He said before He formed us in the womb He already knew us! It just took birthing our purpose to really bring it to fruition.

Chapter Eight
God Will Make You Laugh!

I know there are times when you feel as if you don't have a purpose, or you may feel as if your purpose is so far off. You've watched so many people blossom in their businesses, their ministries, and in life. You sit, and you wonder, "well, what about me?" You begin to settle as opposed to seeking your true purpose in life. You're okay with the job you have now, because it pays the bills, even though you desire to open up your own business but you think it's too much to do that anyway. You're okay with going to that regular church where the pastor preaches watered down messages, Sunday after Sunday. You desire more, but you stay because your grandmother went there, and her mother went there, and your mother still goes there. But, can I tell you that if you allow God to have full reign over your life, and if you seek Him for your purpose and true meaning in life, He'll make it worthwhile? You look at your present and think it's impossible, but can I tell you that God will make you laugh if you allow Him to?

In Genesis chapter 18, we meet Sarai, wife of then Abram. Both are in their old age, without children. But an angel of the Lord told Abram that he and his wife would have a child. Sarai laughed. She laughed because she was already old and past her child-bearing age. I can just imagine her thoughts. "A child? We can't have children because I'm barren, and even if that weren't the case, I'm way past my child-bearing stage. Who does this man think he is? A child? [laugh]" But then the Lord asked her why she laughed.

The same God that blessed Abraham and Sarah with their son Isaac is the same God that can bless and make what seems like the impossible possible for you. He will make you laugh at the thought of ever thinking He cannot do what He says He will do. Like Sarah and Abraham, He will change your name. No longer will you be addressed by what you have been through; depression, abuse, fear, or insecurity. He will give you a new name; you will now be addressed as joy, peace, and love. We've just got to believe that our God can and will do it. The Bible says Faith without works is dead. So, we've got to start working this thing out by putting our faith to work.

When David killed Goliath, it was evident that he was working his faith. All the odds were against him. He was smaller than Goliath. He had no experience in killing men, but only animals that threatened his flock. He had no shield, armour, or sword. Just his sling and a few rocks. But He knew God! He knew that God was his refuge and his help; he worked his faith. We can no longer rely on the physical and settle on our five senses. I remember my husband preaching one Sunday; he said "...the enemy uses our five senses to suggest defeat to us so that we don't walk in the purpose God has for us. He uses what we see, hear, and feel to discourage us. God always has a plan for each of our lives. His plans outweigh ours. He is all-knowing."

When I think about my life and the events that happened, I just have to laugh at the thought of me thinking that I knew what was best for my life. Whenever I tried to make it on my own, I ended up broken and messed up. Then, when I allowed God to put His hands in it, it became a masterpiece. It didn't happen overnight, but the process was beautiful. It just takes us time to realize that God does have our best interest at heart and that He truly desires for us to walk in the destiny that He has laid out for us from the beginning of time. He wants you to experience Him in all His glory. I want you to walk into all that He has promised you in His Word. He wants you to experience peace, love, joy, and happiness. He wants you to succeed at everything that comes your way, but you've got to trust in Him, and believe that He will do what he says! He will make you laugh!

Prayer

Dear God,

    I'm grateful that your word never lies, in Your presence is fullness of joy. I've been granted that joy! I love you, Lord, for giving me peace and comfort. I'm grateful that I can smile and laugh genuinely because I know that you are with me. I know that you are right by my side; I know that no good thing will be withheld from me because I am Yours. I can live life abundantly because of You. So, Father, help me to always be where You are, so that I can always have the joy, peace, and comfort you promised me. Amen.

Chapter Nine

Vulnerable, Again!

I sat on my bed as tears flushed my face. I know she didn't intend on hurting my feelings, she was trying to give me advice. It was my mom. Earlier in the day she shared with me how there were people who asked her why I looked the way I did. My hair was natural, I still had baby weight on, I wasn't wearing makeup and I was still wearing my maternity clothes. I smiled when she told me, but inside I was hurt. So hurt I cried until my stomach felt like I had done at least sixty sit ups. I couldn't believe it. Well, I could but I didn't want to believe that people were watching me and talking about me behind my back. I can admit, I could've thrown on a bit of makeup or wore heels here and there, but truthfully, I was so focused on my babies and their needs. I didn't allow myself to splurge knowing that they needed pampers, milk and clothes. But, I was just so hurt. Chris finally got me to calm down and asked me what was going on. He thought that it was something he had done unknowingly. I explained to him and like any husband, he got defensive and then he allowed God to speak through Him. He asked me whom I was trying to please, and why I allowed the words of the devil to cloud my mind as truth. This was a distraction for me, it came to cause me to focus solely on material things instead of focusing on what God had called me to do. I was so conscious of the words they said to my mother. I became obsessed. I started to order clothes online, and purchase makeup and Remy hair, just because I wanted to show 'them' that I didn't become that person they were talking about. I would scroll through Instagram and Facebook, looking for trends to follow. I started to lose weight, and hearing people say how nice I was looking made me happy. So, there I was, again, faced with insecurity. It never left, it was just suppressed. It showed up big and bold, like when you pluck one grey hair, and another appears. I desired to please people, and I desired to be liked, and feel 'important'.

"No man can serve two masters: for either he will hate the one and love the other, or else, he will hold to the one and despise the other. Ye cannot serve God and mammon." Matthew 6:24.

I wasn't serving God completely if I was allowing the mere words of man to control my actions. I needed to realize that His say was the only say that should matter. I took a step back and asked Him to forgive me for allowing a mere man to control my mind and my actions. As human beings, we desire to be liked, especially as women. We desire affirmation, but the only affirmation that should hold true and firm in our lives should be the word of God. Once we grasp His word that "...I am fearfully and wonderfully made...' Psalm 139:14 we can go through life fully confident in ourselves knowing that God is the ultimate artist of life and He's proven to be perfect at it. He knew us from our mother's womb. He knows our innermost being, and yet He still loves us. Even though you may be struggling with depression, fear, insecurity and your faith in Him; He still loves you and desires for you to know him. "As for God, his way is perfect: The Lord's word is flawless; He shields all who take refuge in him." Psalm 18:30. Knowing the word of God allows you to withstand whatever may come your way. The Bible urges us to hide the word of God in our heart. So whenever we are faced with something we can use His word toward whatever situation we may be going through. We must practice speaking life over ourselves and watch God move on our behalf.

Prayer

Dear God,

In you there is peace, in you there is strength, in you there is joy. Help me to remember that you are all I need when I feel less than what I am. With You, I can fight depression and win; I can fight fear and win, I can fight insecurity and win. In you there is restoration. Restore me oh God. Restore and mend everything that is broken in my life. Amen.

Chapter Ten

The Bounce Back

I wanted to please God. I no longer wanted those people that are also subjected to Him to have a say in my life. I refused to be caught off guard again by the words of the enemy. I realized that I needed to love and see myself the way God does so I started to read more about God's love. "But you, O Lord, are a God merciful and gracious, slow to anger and abounding in steadfast love and faithfulness.' Psalm 86:10.

I started to speak over myself and took steps to walking in victory. I can assure you that it is not easy, especially when you've lived your life wanting to please others and show that you are good enough. It takes so much time and effort to please people. You must keep up with the girl next door, and in doing so, you lose yourself...your true self. So much pressure has been put on us as women; particularly those who are after the heart of God. Social media and television have portrayed women as objects as opposed to being women of substance who have more to offer than their bodies. We've watched women refashion their bodies; their eyes, hips, breasts and lips, all for the sake of being 'accepted,' by this world. Just by their actions, they are naively saying "I don't like how I was created, I do not accept the natural me, it's not enough.' When we start to compare ourselves to others on social media; Snapchat, Instagram, or Facebook, we discredit the God who has created us all unique and beautiful in His eyes. We become carbon copies of those we 'admire' and our identity slips out the door. Our identity sets us apart. No two people have the same identity; everyone is different. Social media has convinced us that our true self is not good enough, so we 'enhance' our bodies and conform to the world and its standard of beauty.

I distinctly remember my husband voicing his opinion on extensions and makeup. He said "I don't understand y'all, why can't women just be natural? Why the heap of makeup and hair that isn't yours?" Of course, I side-eyed him because, at the time, I felt as though I needed the hair, nails, and makeup to feel beautiful and a bit confident; then it became a necessity, a crutch. There are thousands of women in the world who have the same views I had. To them, all those things are essential for them to view themselves as beautiful. There is something so beautiful about a woman who knows her worth and beauty versus someone who is completely lost under the Remy hair, stiletto heels, and the contour lines. As women, we should love and think highly of ourselves, so much that hair, nails, and makeup become an option and not a need. When we go out in public naturally, we should be proud of what we are. We were beautifully created by God, and He only made ONE of you, that alone should ignite our love for our true self. Every day we should wake up knowing that we are beautiful.

Romans 12:2 "Do not copy the behaviour and customs of this world, but let God transform you into a new person by the changing the way you think. Then you will learn to know God's will for you, which is good and pleasing and perfect." The moment I embraced the love God has for me, and His perfect thoughts about me, life became better. I would smile when I see someone whispering about me, or even laugh when I walk into a bustling room and all of a sudden, it goes silent. There are some that may question your confidence, and may suggest that you get with the 'times.' I can hear them right now saying "girl, no one wears those jeans anymore," or "that shirt isn't in style anymore." When you know who you are in Jesus, you'll politely smile and say "those things that are 'in' isn't for me." You have to own yourself, own your confidence and own the words of your Father; He never lies.

Prayer

Dear God,
Thank you for creating me so uniquely—from my physical features to my character. Thank you for being so loving and gracious toward me even when it's hard to love myself. I'm grateful that you find me lovable. I am grateful that you are always so faithful to your words. Sweet Jesus, continue to love on me as I begin to embrace your love for me. Amen.

Chapter Eleven

Guarding Your Heart and Mind

It's so easy to become so consumed with life and what may be going on around us. We may find ourselves being bombarded daily with what's on the news, tragic events taking place all over the world, reality T.V shows that sugar coat sin and subtly say that 'it's okay.' Proverbs 4:23 urges us to guard our hearts with all diligence because out of our hearts flows the issues of life.

Truth be told, life is not easy, especially for us saved women, whether single, engaged or married. Our lives are not textbooks where we can go to page 150 and see how to overcome certain situations. But the word of God tells us to guard it; to guard our hearts.

I remember vividly a few years back when I started to watch basketball wives. This show was filled with 'trophy girlfriends/wives,' drama and cursing. I think I had watched a full season of the show when I began to say words they'd say on the show unconsciously. There were words like 'legit and bougie' I adopted and used regularly. Then the curse words started to leave my lips. At first, I didn't understand what was going on and why I was suddenly 'changing.' I remember praying to God, and the Holy Spirit whispered "you are no longer guarding your heart, so whatever you watch and see are seeds sown, and they're growing. Guard your heart, my daughter." I was driving at the time, and without a second thought, I knew I had to stop watching and listening to things that did not edify my spirit. Reality T.V does not edify my spirit, nor does songs by Nicki Minaj, Beyoncé or Rihanna. They tug at your spirit and cause you to think solely about what they are singing about, especially if it's on repeat, and their songs are NOT talking about Jesus. Worldly music and shows feed your flesh, that is all. We cannot and should not do what the world does. Therefore, we cannot watch or participate in things that do not glorify our God. Colossians 3:2 says "Set your affection on things above, not on the things of this earth." Our focus should never be on worldly things. We are in this world, but we are certainly not of this world. Guarding our hearts calls for prayer, firstly. Our prayer every day should be asking God to help us keep Him first in everything we do. It's so important to understand that we really do need Him; we cannot survive this world without His grace and mercy. Guarding our hearts also requires for us to know His word inside and out and to become familiar with it. David says in Psalm 119:11 "I have hidden your word in my heart, that I might not sin against you." It took me a while to grasp this, even though I had heard it time after time. When trouble and situations arise, we can quote the word of God which is sharp and precise, toward whatever we're dealing with. We can speak to the spirit of depression, sickness, and poverty all from

His word alone. He reminds us that life and death lie in our tongue. We have the power to create life-filled situations, But, we can only do that if we've got the word of God hidden in our hearts and use it in our everyday lives. We will never be defeated once the word of God is rooted and grounded in our hearts.

Prayer

Heavenly Father,

Psalm 119 reminds me that your word is a lamp unto my feet and a light unto my path. Lord, let me always remember Your word when things come my way, big or small. I desire for your word be so rooted in me, oh Lord, that I never forget even during the hardest times in my life. Let your Spirit reign in my life, let your presence take over my life. Let my life be the perfect picture of your grace and mercy. Let my testimony be an example to those who need to know that your grace is still real, that your grace still heals, that your grace still delivers! Oh, Jesus! Right now, let me have clean hands and a pure heart toward you, let it always be about

You! Create in me a clean heart, Jesus, as my mind remains on you, and as my heart lean towards you. In your precious name, Amen.

Chapter Twelve

The Cross

When we say yes to Jesus and His will for our lives, we must be willing to take up the cross He too took up for us. There is the misconception that when we become Christians, our lives are perfect and that we never encounter tests and trials. Our lives are always being challenged to walk like Christ, think like Christ, and respond to situations as Christ did. Matthew 16:24 "Then Jesus said to his disciples, if any of you wants to be my follower, you must turn from your selfish ways, take up your cross, and follow me." NIV When I read this, my mind went directly to when I gave my life to Him. At the time, I thought that

I had given Him all, but I had only given Him some of me, and not all. You see there were things I still held on to, for instance before I got married, my now husband and I struggled with fornication, but we were 'saved.' There were also things I desired for my life, but I hadn't consulted God for His will; again, not giving my all. There are so many things I can list that I did or did not do, but I was saved and claiming to follow Jesus. The title of knowing Him at the point was just enough. Going to Sunday church service, hearing tear-jerking songs, and falling out was just enough for me. I thought I was hitting the mark, but I was so far off. That was not all He required of me. He required ALL of me. He required my heart, my soul, my very existence. I had to get to the point where He became ALL I desired and ALL I needed. I think that some of us at one point in our Christian walk failed to give God all of us. Don't get me wrong, we all like the idea of 'giving God all of us,' but the action behind it sometimes escapes us. Truth be told, giving Him all of you means you won't move without His say, and that His say is the first and final say to whatever questions or ideas we may have about our lives. With everything in our lives, we ought to consult Him and wait patiently, without complaint or grumbling, for His answer. Before you take that job, consult Him. Before you move from one place to another, consult Him. God desires a real relationship with us. He doesn't just sit on His throne, bark orders at us and we file in one straight line. No. He desires a relationship where we can just come to Him with anything, and we can receive comfort in knowing that He's got our best interest at heart. If I told you that God desires for you to prosper in everything you do, would you believe me, wholeheartedly? Are you able to believe that every situation you've encountered has a purpose attached to it, whether it came to teach you the art of patience, or remind you of God's unfailing love? I need you to believe that your situation is not the end of the world, and that purpose is not just for a selected few. The fact that you're reading this book signifies that there is a mustard seed size of faith deep down in you, paired with hope, that just maybe your pain has a purpose.

Often, as women, we over analyse every situation that we may be faced with. We give logistics more credit that the power of the God we claim to serve. He's the same God who remembered Hannah, Rachael, Sarah and opened their wombs. He's the same God that granted favour to Esther and Rahab, need I go on? Nothing is impossible with God. He is the all possible, no situation is too hard for Him, and no situation can come as a surprise to Him. The cross that we're designed to carry as Christians resembles the same cross that Jesus bore some thousand years ago. Saying "yes" means that you will be persecuted and sometimes labelled an outcast for what you believe in. There are some people who will listen to you as you tug on their hearts with the gospel, and then there may be some who will shun you for just mentioning the name "Jesus." The most beautiful thing about carrying the cross with Jesus is sharing your testimony, wholeheartedly and truthfully. There may be people who take your testimony and use it negatively, but I can assure you that percentage is less than the number of people that are grateful that you took the step to share just how God delivered you. You see, sometimes it takes for them to see just how unworthy and covered in sin you were to realize that grace is real and that it saves even the most wretched soul. Sometimes it takes coming out of the four walls and sitting with the girl on the corner and opening up about your life of sin so that she can realize that salvation is not farfetched. Sometimes it takes coming off your high horse to sit with those that view themselves as low to hug on them and love on them. Show them your vulnerability, show them your strength through grace. They need it; this is the symbol of the cross. His cross symbolizes grace, His unfailing love, hope, peace, and life. So, when we say yes, we pick up our cross, there is no doubt about that. The comfort we have is that He gives us the grace to bear the cross. On our own, we cannot survive without His grace and His peace. This world is getting darker and darker, but He soothes us with His presence and His word.

Prayer

Even though the world is getting darker and darker, you, oh Lord, are my comfort. You are a shelter and refuge for all who trust in You. You are my provider and my protector; there is no other name than the name of Jesus that man can call on and be saved. In you, there is hope. We put our trust in you, Lord, because you will deliver us from whatever may come our way. Even as we take up our crosses to follow You, we do it with gratefulness, because you paid the ultimate price for us. Give us the strength to be who you've called us to be. Help us to be the beacon of light for those who may be hurting around us. Amen.

Chapter Thirteen

The Butterfly Effect

The butterfly is undoubtedly one of the most beautiful creatures God has created on this earth. To many, it depicts the glory of God in our lives. For the butterfly to become the beautiful creature that it is, it goes through stages. Some stages take weeks and then there are some that take years, depending on the butterfly and the environment it's in. I compare both our natural and spiritual walk to the stages of a butterfly.

We're caterpillars when we don't have it all together; when we're covered in sin, and ugly from the effects of it. We're caterpillars when we don't know which way we're going and when we don't have enough faith to see where we can possibly go. At this stage, some of us find ourselves at a standstill, so confused with the world around us. Here, we just go with the flow. The world ends up dictating to us what we should do, what we should wear, how we should act; all because we don't know who we are and the authority we possess. During this time, we are in no hurry to find our purpose, because we think we have none.

Then there is the Chrysalis stage, here is where beauty overrides our negative thinking and surpasses the thoughts the world has about us. Here is where we allow God to work. Right here is where we shed the sin, insecurities, and fear to make way for growing wings. At this moment, God whispers in our ears; He sheds light on the possibility of trusting Him and allowing Him to lead and guide our lives. At this point, our 'maybes' and our uncertainties are overpowered by the strength we've gained through spending quality time with Jesus. We're gearing up for the world around us, we're coming out stronger and better, with the hope that no longer will we be defeated with Jesus as the captain of our sails.

Then, we emerge. We emerge with a whole new look on life. We emerge with joy, peace, long-suffering, love, and meekness. We come out with His word engrafted in our hearts and our minds. We are free, no longer captives to sin. Our purpose is now clear, whether it is to speak in front of thousands or even minister to people one at a time about the grace of God. He's graced you from the very beginning. He is the Alpha, the Omega, the beginning, and the end; He is the first, the middle, and the last. He is the El Shaddai, the Lord God Almighty. Nothing catches Him by surprise. He knew you, even before you began to know yourself. He is just that good. Will you trust Him? Will you trust in His ability to be all-knowing? Will you trust Him and His track record of never failing? Will you trust that He will keep you in perfect peace? Will you trust that He knows what's best for you? His grace is all sufficient, all powerful, all encompassing. His grace restores our souls and leads us in the way of righteousness. I have no doubt that God wants us to flourish…in Him. He's not rooting for our failure, but He's rooting for us to prosper. He is rooting for us to obey His commandments. He's rooting for us to build a relationship with Him. We are His disciples; we are His Bride. He's given so much to us; we have tangible evidence of how amazing His love is for us. The beauty of a butterfly, beyond a shadow of a doubt, would be its wings and the colours that don it. The beauty of yours would be that even though you've struggled, whether it be an addiction, coping with abuse, or whatever hardships that maybe in your past, you've learnt how to trust Jehovah. You've learnt how to rely on Him fully. He is no longer an option for your day to day living—He is now a necessity to survive. He has now become your all in all.

Prayer

Dear God,

I realize that my broken pieces aren't a curse, once you're in the midst. I thank you for allowing me to be broken so that you can come and heal what needs to be mended in my life. I thank you for your grace right now that is overshadowing me. I thank you for your peace, your joy, and most importantly, your love for me. Without it, I would remain broken. Thank you for not casting me away when I call. Thank You for piecing together those broken pieces. I no longer look like what I've been through. I'm now adorned in grace, love, peace, joy, long-suffering, and I've gained wings of freedom; in You there is liberty. I've been liberated; I'm no longer bound to sin, mistakes or the words or my enemies. Amen

Conclusion

I had no idea what was in store for my life; I realized I was never in charge, to begin with. I could plan as much as I could, but He had the ultimate say. I must admit that my plans and my thoughts would never measure up to how incredible His plans were for my life, but back then I couldn't understand it. Even though I had found myself taking on water, I still tried to row without Him. I still tried to do it my way. Isn't that crazy? No matter how deep you may be, or how stubborn and disgruntled you may find yourself, He still throws you the rope to pull you into safety. He still comes in and puts together all those broken parts of you that you've managed to shatter into a thousand pieces. It doesn't matter where we're at; He just wants us to trust and believe in Him. He wants us to believe that even though we may be struggling to build a relationship with Him, or even though we haven't prayed or read His word in a while, He still loves us and has a purpose for our lives.

If truth be told, He's always fighting for us. He's never stopped. When death and harsh judgement should be our portion, because of our sins, he says 'I bled for her sins. I bled for that abortion she committed that no one knows about. I bled for all those times she committed adultery and fornication…' You see, He knows our beginning, our middle and our end. He knows everything about us and still, He desires to commune with us, even when the world has labelled us broken, damaged and confused. He desires for us to realize just how much He loves us when the 'perfect church' has dubbed us unfit. In my heart of hearts, I believe that we are beautifully graced for this journey called life.

Psalm 139:2 -5 "…You know my thoughts before I think them, you know where I go and where I lie down. You know everything I do. Lord, even before I say a word, you already know it. You are all around me—in front and in back—and you have put your hand on me." This scripture is so profound, so beautiful, and so comforting. Through every situation, every trial, every high and low in our lives, He has always shadowed us. He was always there to sprinkle His grace over us, even when we didn't know. Even those times we couldn't feel, see or hear Him, His grace was present. The little flicker of hope that pushed us, the little spurts of strength we felt, was all Him, all His way of gracing us for what we were experiencing. Don't get weary, don't faint! Isaiah 40:29 "He gives strength to the weary and increases the power of the weak." We have been beautifully graced, my sister; graced to take on this world, graced to share the love of the incredible God that has loved us back to life. So, I salute you, you graced beauty, as you journey to your destiny, to your purpose, to finding your true self through God. I salute you for making up your mind that life without Him is hard and empty. I salute you because grace now has a new meaning in your life. For your journey, for your hardships, for your trials, you have been beautifully graced.

About the Author

Ashley J Darling is a woman who is primarily committed to her love of Christ and family. Her values are beyond substantial because of her passion for the things of Christ. She is an eminent mother of two, wife, sister, daughter and friend. Strength and grace woven throughout her veins, she walks the path of righteousness being a beacon of light to not only those who come after her but those who are present and before her. The strength of her character is not shaken and is sturdy with ethical morals that prove that she is a God-fearing woman of intellect and outstanding stature.

About the Book

Being a Christian does not mean that we are exempt from trials, nor does it mean that our lives are picture perfect. Ashley knows of this oh too well. In this book, she finds herself wrestling with depression and anxiety during her Christian walk. Once upon a time, she hid her struggle behind the cliché of the 'perfect Christian.' She knows what it's like to feel trapped behind what's expected of you versus confronting your truth. In this book, she gives it all over to God; the desire to be perfect for mere man, and allows God's grace to take over her life in a way like never before. Her journey to grace has strengthened her relationship with God and has propelled her into her destiny. She is a firm believer of God's grace and unconditional love. No matter what broken pieces you may be holding, you're never too far from God. He is always there to restore you. Amazing things happen when grace takes over

Facebook: Ashley Jordan Darling

Instagram: ashley.jordan.d

Snap Chat: ashleyjordan55

www.ingramcontent.com/pod-product-compliance
Lightning Source LLC
Chambersburg PA
CBHW071148090426
42736CB00012B/2268